ⓑ Many instructors prefer 1 4 2 3 1 4 2 3.

@ The realization of the trills in this movement represents the minimum number of repercussions. Each trill may have more repercussions. The notes of the suffix should be played at the same speed as those in the trill.

The following note appears at the top of the first page of the original edition: "N. B. Out of the VARIOUS MODES of fingering the SAME PASSAGE, the Author has preferred THAT, which appeared to him the best calculated to form the hand of a beginner."

Sonatina in C

Muzio Clementi (1752–1832)
(Opus 36, No. 1)

 Many piano instructors prefer 4 2 3 1 4 2 3 1 4 2 1.

Cover art: The Old Burgtheater in Vienna, 1783
by Carl Schütz (Austrian, 1745–1800)
Colored etching
Historisches Museum Stadt Wien, Vienna, Austria
Erich Lessing/Art Resource, New York

CLEMENTI

SONATINA IN C   OPUS 36, NO. 1

EDITED BY WILLARD A. PALMER

AN ALFRED MASTERWORK EDITION

© The suffix does not appear in the original edition, but Clementi makes it clear in his INTRODUCTION TO THE ART OF PLAYING ON THE PIANOFORTE that it should generally be added whether it is shown or not, when the symbol *tr* is used.

Vivace

ⓐ Most editions have **p** . The **pp** starting the recapitulation (measure 35) suggests the same dynamics should be used at the beginning of the movement, especially in view of the fact that all other dynamics in the recapitulation correspond to those of the first statement.

ⓑ The fingering of the right hand in the original edition is 2 5 1. We suggest 2 4 1, as in measure 3.

Alfred

2159   USA

ISBN 0-7390-0843-9